ESSENTIAL

FASHION
ILLUSTRATION
COLOR + MEDIUM

ROCKPORT

ESSENTIAL

FASHION
ILLUSTRATION
COLOR + MEDIUM

BEVERLY MASSACHUSETTS

ROCKPORT

PUBLISHERS

Copyright © 2008 by **maomao** publications
First published in 2008 in the United States of America by
Rockport Publishers, a member of
Quayside Publishing Group
33 Commercial Street
Gloucester, MA 01930-0589
Telephone: (978) 282-9590
Fax: (978) 283-2742
www.rockpub.com

ISBN-13: 978-1-59253-430-2
ISBN-10: 1-59253-430-9

10 9 8 7 6 5 4 3 2 1

Publisher: Paco Asensio
Editorial coordination: Anja Llorella Oriol
Text edition: Macarena San Martín
Art director: Emma Termes Parera
Layout: Maira Purman
Photography: Gogortza & Llorella
English translation: Jay Noden

Editorial project:
maomao publications
Tallers, 22 bis, 3º 1ª
08001 Barcelona, Spain
Tel.: +34 93 481 57 22
Fax: +34 93 317 42 08
www.maomaopublications.com

Printed in China

Contents

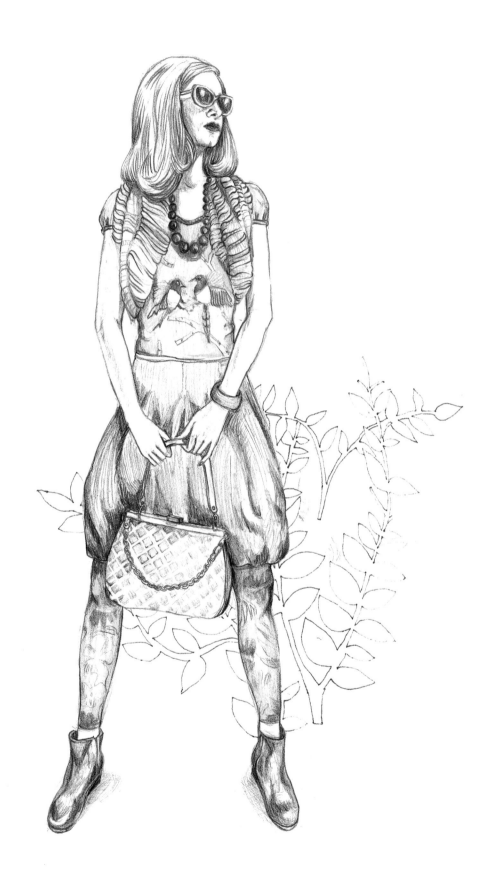

Introduction

Fashion illustration is a fundamental tool for presenting a designer's creations. Not only does it need to be an aesthetically pleasing image, but also it likely has to provide certain information and show certain qualities of the clothing. When sketching a new creation a fashion designer will most likely not draw a hyper-realistic illustration, but instead is more likely to produce an image with exaggerated proportions, an idealized silhouette which shows off the garment's main characteristics. However, to be able to do this first and foremost it is necessary to know how to illustrate. This is why it is important to know how to use the different techniques that exist for transferring the properties and characteristics of a given item of clothing onto paper. Since the aim of fashion illustration is to represent the design in the best way possible, it is fundamental to take into account what material the garment is made of when deciding which techniques to employ. Each material has a different texture, some materials are shiny, like satin, others opaque, like linen, some are semi-transparent, like tulle, and others are thicker, like felt. These different textures affect the perception of the color. White satin, for example, does not have the same appearance as white wool, and black leather is not the same as black cotton. Each of these examples will be better represented, according to their texture and perception of color, by way of a different technique.

As a guide to setting out in the field of fashion illustration, this book teaches readers how to use five of the most classic techniques: pencils, watercolors, pastels, gouache, and markers. Each of these is developed by a different illustrator, all of whom are professionals with close links to the world of fashion. Step-by-step, didactic exercises show how to apply the technique in question, each of their different qualities, and the different methods that exist to attain different and varied results. The illustration of a figure dressed in an outfit constitutes a final exercise for each of the techniques. Consequently, as well as seeing how an illustration can vary from one technique to another, an array of different illustration styles can also be appreciated: the same task given to five different illustrators may result in five totally different illustrations. As an accessory to these techniques, the final chapter of this book visually explores other forms of illustration, both digital and hand produced.

Pencil

Pencil is is the most basic and traditional of drawing mediums, and has become universal thanks to its versatility and accessibility. Its use can help achieve illustrations with a high level of detail and it is ideal for representing volumes, shadows, lights, and highlights in a picture. It is easy to erase, allowing it to be used as a base for drawing, regardless of the technique used afterwards for applying color. There are two types of leads, soft and hard. Soft pencils—identified with the letter B (B for black)—produce a very dark line, making them fundamental for creating black areas, and provide a higher degree of flexibility and expression. The hard leads—known as H from hard—are dryer and grayish in tone; they produce a finer, lighter line, so they are often used for sketches and for detail work. There are also pencils with lots of different color leads, although to learn to use them and master the technique, for example combining them and controlling the intensity of the line, it is best to start with just the basic colors—cyan, yellow, and magenta.

Tamara Villoslada

Tamara was born in 1977 in the town of Esquel, in Argentinean Patagonia. After several moves she eventually arrived in Cordoba, where she studied art and communication science and formed part of the Bistró Casares multidisciplinary group. In 2002 she decided to move to Barcelona, where she directed her career in art toward illustration, after having completed a postgraduate course in the Escuela Eina. Her illustrations have been published in magazines all over the world. She has designed T-shirts for the Japanese brand Graniph and illustrated objects for Poketo (Los Angeles and Japan)—work that was exhibited in Barcelona's Duduá store. In the publishing sector, her most recent project was to illustrate *El templo de la ciencia* for the publishing house Editorial Planeta.

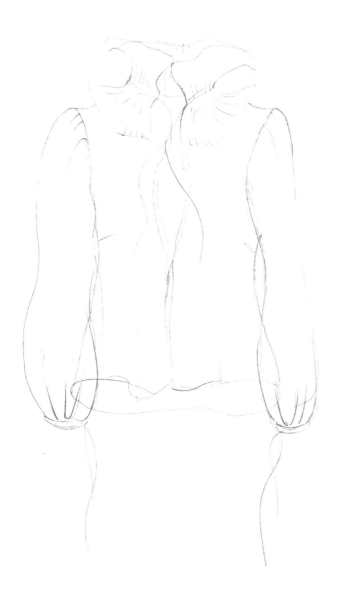

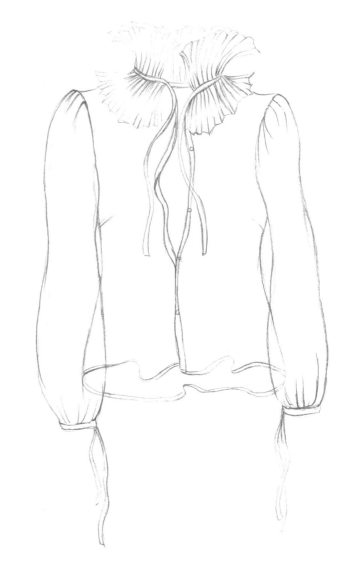

Sketches are made of the possible ways to express the qualities of this blouse with a pleated collar. Since the blouse in this case displays transparencies and is made from particularly fine fabric, showing it loose—on a hanger for example—accentuates its lightweight, delicate appearance.

The lines that are not going to be used are cleaned, and a pencil of medium hardness is used to draw the details of the blouse. The folds of the collar are outlined, taking into account the way in which the neck falls in order to strengthen its real volume and perspective.

Finally, the light and shadow are defined. Special care must be taken for the areas of transparency, where the different overlapping layers and textures must be perceived. These areas can be darker, thereby simulating a greater concentration of material.

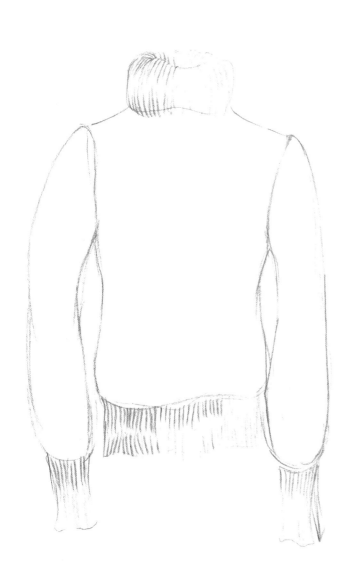

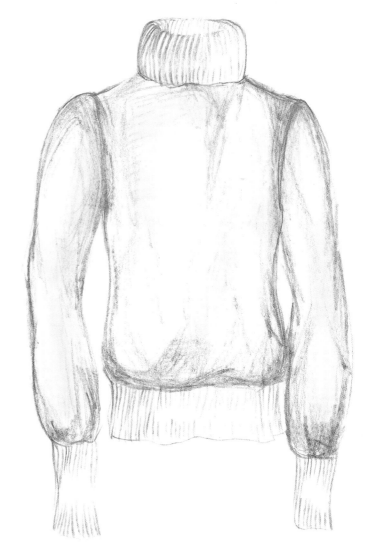

Since color will be the most prominent feature of this illustration, a graphite pencil is not used to sketch the garment. It is done directly with color—with a special color pencil, which is easily erased—so that afterward these lines integrate easily with the final drawing.

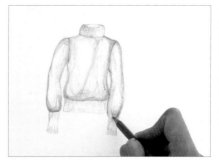

With the same color pencil the pattern for the rest of the jersey is drawn. The volume of the garment must be taken into account and how this affects the design; the pattern becomes narrower at the sides and wider in the middle.

Once all the colors have been applied, the lines are strengthened by applying more pressure where the pattern requires more presence, like in the middle section or the parts with shading. Gently applying color creates volume, while also respecting the pattern.

A figure is sketched in a pose that shows off the skirt. Given the volume and the fall of the garment, a three-quarters position is chosen. The general lines of the skirt and the main folds formed by the volume are sketched with a hard pencil (2H).

The figure is outlined and the details of the skirt start to take shape. The rest of the clothing must be simple to avoid visually competing with the item being shown. The line that outlines the figure should be left as clean and defined as possible.

The shadows are drawn, first through areas sketched with a medium pencil (HB), which allows us to test the effects of the chiaroscuro and the volumes. The finish is done with a propelling pencil, which, thanks to its sharp end, offers greater precision.

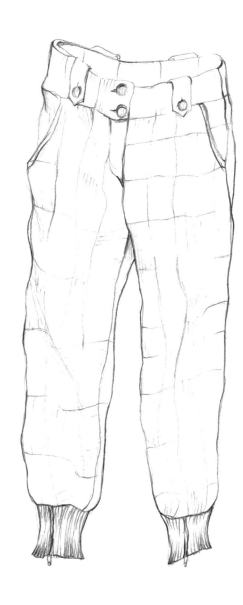

A sketch is done of the trousers in movement, to represent the pattern in a more realistic way. Details such as the waistline, buttons, pockets, and belt loops are drawn, and the texture of the trouser cuffs is also represented.

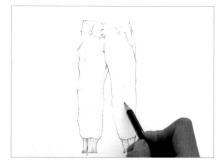

The checks are drawn with a delicate line, which is easy to erase (2H pencil). It is important to take special care to respect the folds in the fabric. The lines of the pattern appear, disappear, and fold in these areas.

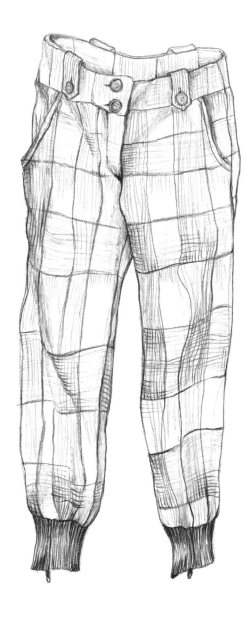

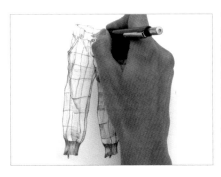

The lines in areas where there is more shade are strengthened and the details are finished with greater accuracy. With a soft lead propelling pencil (B type) high definition can be achieved even in dark areas where the line seems to overlap with what's behind.

The figure is drawn in an appropriate posture for showing the coat. A frontal pose allows the viewer to appreciate the details. The volume of the coat and the main lines are sketched and the figure is given boots, which do not interfere with the ensemble.

The figure, which has taken shape from the previous sketches, is outlined. The details of the coat, the main creases, and faint shading are drawn. Representing the highlights will be fundamental in demonstrating the quality of the polished material.

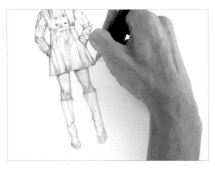

Different quality pencils are used and areas are left white. With soft pencils (3 or 4B) bold strokes are used to achieve almost completely black areas, which contrast with the areas left white, which represent the shine of the leather.

This coat can also be done in color, since in this case it is the strong contrast in shades that gives the garment its character. Creating bright reds and still leaving other areas white, will achieve the same shiny effect.

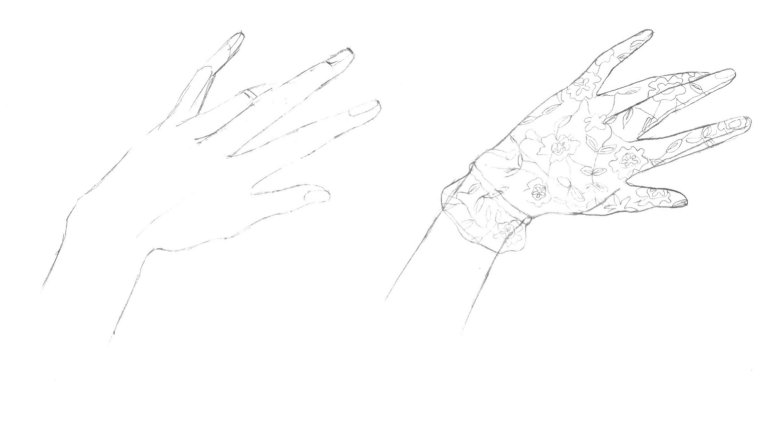

Different sketches of the hand are drawn to find a position that is visually attractive. Since the fabric has a lot of texture and details, when the hand is more outstretched these characteristics of the glove can be better appreciated.

A hard pencil (2H) is used to draw the first details of the lace, since this is the initial sketch. The pattern is added to, taking into account the hand's morphology, the indents, and folds. Once the outline has been defined, the lines are strengthened with an HB pencil.

Volume is given to the glove by coloring with different pencils, from HB for the more transparent areas up to 3 or 4B to achieve the darker sections. Keep in mind, the level of darkness of the different pencils also depends on the pressure applied.

The hat is begun by way of a reasonably detailed initial sketch. It is important to bear in mind that the texture of the material of the hat and the volume of its flower need to be seen. This is why the best option is to do an initial drawing.

The edges of the hat are defined using a pencil of medium hardness. The details are outlined and textures—of the hat, hair and mouth—added, always considering the light, in this case from above, and the areas of shadow that this will form.

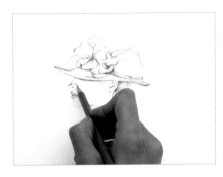

Pencils of different hardness generate levels of darkness, which give the hat structure, leaving areas of sharp contrast, which better define the figure. Special attention is paid to the volume of the flower, exaggerating a little to allow it to stand out in the composition.

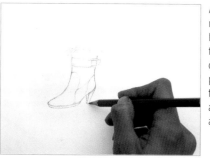

A sketch of the boot is done, marking the main elements like the heel, buckle, cuts of the leather, and the texture of the fur. Quick and accurate pencil strokes are used for this, which begin strongly as they come from the boot, and weaken toward the end.

Once the figure has been defined, the line is cleaned—with the help of an eraser—and the definitive lines are drawn in. Greater pressure is applied to the pencil in order to obtain a firm, defined stroke. The shading is added using different levels of darkness.

The gradient shading depends on the frontal-lateral light that this boot receives. For the hairs, a propelling pencil is used since this provides a finer line; it is recommendable to combine leads of different hardness to achieve darker or grayer tones.

Sketches are done to define the figure. Once chosen, the figure of the girl with the clothes on is insinuated. It is drawn with light strokes made with a very hard pencil so that after the lines are erased and the drawing is left clean.

The different garments are drawn on the figure with certain details, including the creases of the waistcoat, the shirr of the sleeves, the highlight from the glasses, the facial expression, the creases of the Boulloné skirt, the sole, and shading of the boots, etc.

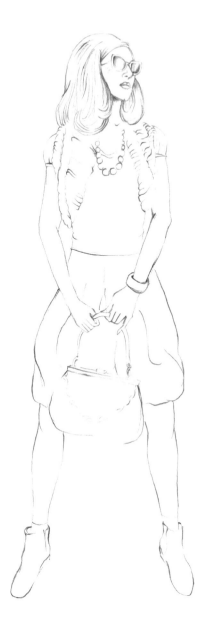

In this step the figure is outlined more firmly and with a clean line, using a medium hard pencil (HB). More pressure is applied for areas where there is more shading or definition and the pencil line is weaker in light areas, in order to suggest volume and light.

The first details are drawn, without adding the light or shading. The details of the shirt pattern and the motifs on the leggings are then drawn, paying special attention to the projection of the different textures.

The volumes are modeled through darker and lighter gray areas. The areas of shading are determined and spaces are left white for the highlights, thereby creating gradient shading. To create intense blacks a B pencil is used.

A color is integrated into the composition so that it does not appear excessively monotonous. Since the gray from the graphite dominates the composition, it is important to carefully choose the areas where color will be applied so that it is not lost, which may happen if it is applied to a dark area.

Color is also applied to the bracelet and leggings, depending on the volume of the leg and without considering their pattern. Greater contrast is achieved between the tones of garments like the skirt and the boots, in order to enhance their body and denote the volume.

The last step is to go over the final details with a propelling pencil, which allows for more detailed work. To finish the composition, an extra touch of color is added as decoration and to give the composition personality, without taking anything away from the figure.

Watercolors

This is a technique of painting with colors diluted in water. The colors used are transparent, and their opacity depends on the amount of water used to mix them. These colors can be found in various formats, such as tubes, blocks, watercolor pencils, and as liquids. The most common support for working with this technique is paper. With the wide variety available, the most adequate is one that has a higher basis weight than normal paper, which can be found in different textures and colors. The tool most often used to apply it is the brush. Due to the

way in which they are employed, the use of watercolors offers many possibilities, such as even washes, color overlaps, and gradation. It is also possible to create different effects with different application methods, such as with a sponge or scraper. Thanks to these characteristics, it is the ideal technique for representing transparencies and light fabrics, such as silk or gauze.

Verónica Ballart

From a very early age Verónica Ballart (Stockholm, 1979) felt a strong inclination toward drawing and fashion. Her first studies focused on graphic design, after which she moved to Barcelona—where her mother was born—to continue the same degree in the design school IDEP. Her work placement in the graphics department of Mango presented her with the opportunity to apply her designs to T-shirts. Due to her high standard of work, she continued at the company for a year after having finished the placement. Following this she worked for Incites, a fashion design studio, creating graphics and illustrations for clothing. Today she works as a freelance graphic designer and illustrator, collaborating with various brands and companies. Her inspiration comes from her travels, the street, books, and magazines.

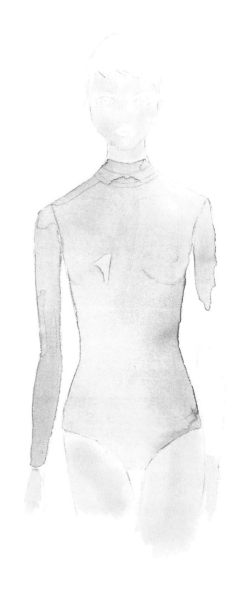

First the figure is drawn with a pencil, without too much attention to detail. Before color is added, the area of paper that will be painted on is moistened with a brush. After waiting a few minutes the skin tone can be applied to the entire body, including the top.

Once dry, the top is painted in a light shade, in this case gray, and a fairly diluted layer is applied so that the skin color is still perceptible. It is recommendable to use few brushstrokes, in order to avoid the brush leaving water marks.

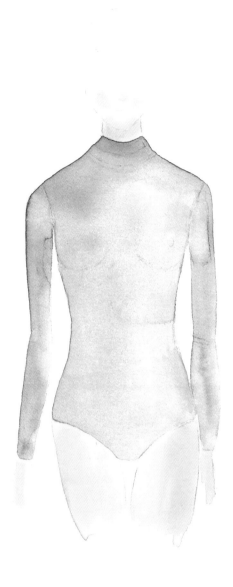

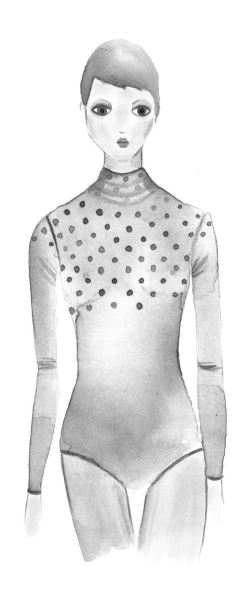

Shading is created to donate the volumes and emphasize folds and creases. To do this, various layers in darker shades are applied, which are painted over the whole body, including the top. To create a greater variety of texture, different tones are used.

The last step is to paint in the details of the illustration. To do this, a fairly undiluted watercolor is used, which is applied with a fine brush that allows small elements to be painted like the polka dots, folds in the arms, edges of the top, eyes, and mouth, etc.

The first step is to draw the figure with a propeller pencil. In this case, not only is the outline is drawn, but also the pattern on the blouse and details like buttons, folds, or flounces, which will make it easier to then apply color.

With a liquid watercolor and a medium-thick brush, the base color of the blouse is evenly applied. The area of the pattern is left white, since this will be done in a different range of colors. Once the base color is painted, it is left to dry completely.

For the pattern, a fine brush is used that allows for a greater level of detail. First the lighter colors are evenly applied—the pink in the flowers and the brown of the branches—and over them the details and the shading are added using colors like violet and gray.

The garment is drawn in detail with a pencil. The area of the paper where color will be applied is moistened and, after waiting until it is almost dry, the first layer can be applied evenly and with a fairly diluted watercolor. This helps to achieve greater texture.

Various layers are applied in different tones of each color, with the aim of forming the different volumes. It is important to take into account the direction of the light in the drawing to create shadows where they are needed and leave the areas that receive most light white.

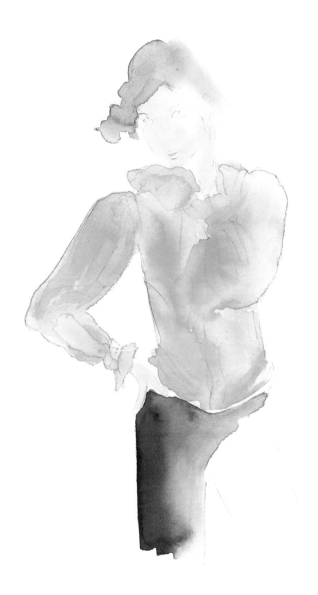

Once various layers have been applied with colors that are darker than the base, a cotton swab is used on the wet watercolor to spread out the quantity of paint. This achieves greater control over the volumes, lights, highlights, and shading.

Once the desired volume is achieved, darker colors are applied—dark blue and black. These are used for the final details, such as the folds, creases, and buttons. A fine brush will afford the work greater accuracy.

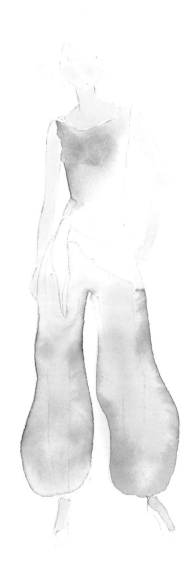

The first step is to draw the figure in pencil. Because the material is transparent, it is necessary to draw the silhouette of the legs, as well as the outline of the trousers, as the legs can be seen through the cloth. The folds and knots in the fabric are also drawn.

With a thick brush, a first layer of color is applied in the softest tone found on the garment. When using a thick brush on a small surface, it is important to be very careful to avoid mixing the different colors.

In order to clearly show that it is a semi-transparent material, the area corresponding to the legs is painted in a darker tone than that of the base of the trousers. The first shading is also applied with this darker tone.

With a darker color (lilac) and a fine brush, the volumes, folds, and creases of the trousers are formed. To do this, the position of the legs is not taken into consideration, and the trousers are considered as a whole. Color is also applied to the area where the legs are.

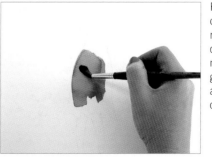

First of all, draw the outline of the skirt with a pencil. It is not necessary to draw the details, but only to mark the main folds of the cloth, as a guide for applying color. After a first layer of color, the base color of the skirt is applied.

The first volumes are created by applying various layers of different colors within the same range, which also enrich the texture. The central area receives most light and should therefore be left lighter than the others.

The last step is to paint the pattern onto the dry skirt. This is done with a very fine brush and a reasonably thick watercolor. For the white details it is better to use gouache, since white watercolor is very difficult to see when applied over darker colors.

The coat and all its details, like buttons, belt, pockets, folds, etc., are drawn in pencil. With a fine brush a "liquid mask" is applied over the lights and details of the coat, which, when finished, are meant to be lighter.

Once the liquid mask has dried, the coat is painted. To do this, color is applied to all of the coat's surface in a light shade of brown, with a fairly diluted watercolor. It is not a problem to paint over the mask.

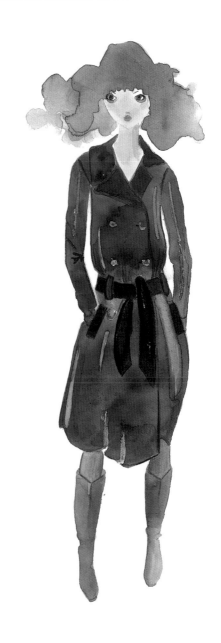

Different layers are applied with different mixes of browns. A thick watercolor is used, since this will help to create the effect of the skin. Also, to accentuate this effect, it is important to wait for each layer to dry before applying another.

Carefully take off the mask with a craft knife or tweezers. To avoid damage, the mask should not be left on for too long. Once it is taken off completely, the areas are painted in a light tone, so that the details and the lights stand out.

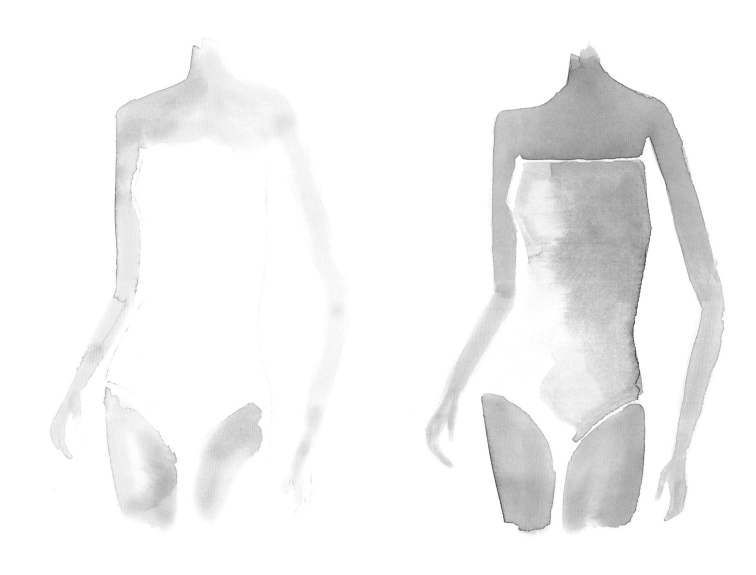

A fine-pointed soft pencil is used to draw the figure with the bathing suit, marking the draping on the chest. With a medium brush, the paper is lightly moistened with water on the drawn figure. Once this is almost dry, a skintone is applied to the body.

The next step is to color the bathing suit. Begin with a very pale and diluted gray, taking into account the direction of the light. Because in this case, it is coming from the left-hand side, fewer layers are applied on that side so it appears brighter.

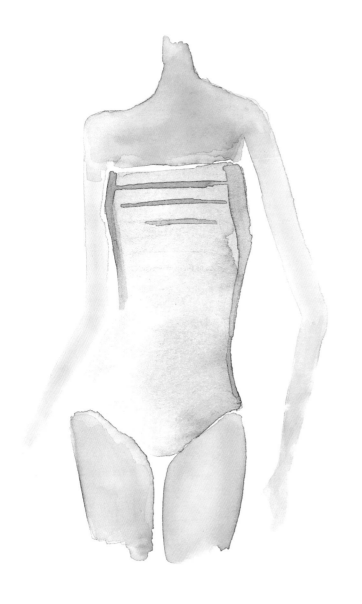

Once the base is colored and while it is still wet, the volumes are created with a less diluted, darker shade of gray. A fine brush is used for this, marking the folds that are formed by the draping on the chest, as well as the shading on the bathing suit.

The last step is adding the details; the creases and the outline are painted with an almost black-gray to better define the figure. To incorporate a little color, bracelets are painted, applying the diluted color directly onto the skin.

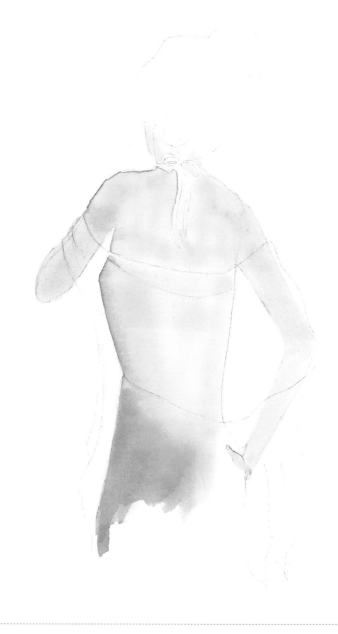

To better appreciate the transparency of the shawl, the figure is drawn from the back. This is done in pencil, marking the main folds and overlaps of the fabric as well as the outline. Then the skin is given a faint color, including the areas that the shawl covers.

Next, the dress is given color. This is done first with very diluted layers of pink, which gradually create volume. As was the case with the skin, the area of the dress covered by the shawl is also given color to achieve the effect of transparency.

Color is applied to the shawl with a thick brush. In the areas where it covers the skin or the dress, it appears darker, and where it is alone, lighter. For greater control, it is recommendable to work with a reasonably diluted watercolor and apply several layers.

The details are painted using a finer brush. The creases and folds of the shawl are marked with a darker shade of gray, following the fall and movement of the material. Color is applied to the dress tie and the hair, and the shadows are added to create the volumes.

With a pencil the figure is drawn with all its details, from folds and creases to the shapes from the pattern or the texture of the bag and jersey. The surface of the paper that will be used is moistened and left until it is almost dry.

The first coloring is applied to the skin, the lightest tone of the composition. Then, working with a diluted watercolor, the base color of the jersey is painted carefully and evenly in a light shade of gray.

Then, the shirt, skirt, leggings, bag, and hair, which receive an initial faint, diluted layer of color. The combination of the colors begins to give volume to the figure and to create a composition.

For the details of the garment a finer brush and a darker tone than that of the garment itself are used, with a slightly more diluted watercolor. The folds, creases, and edges of the clothes are marked, and the pattern of the shirt is drawn.

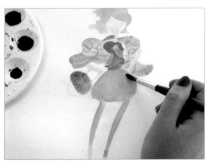

To enhance the volume of the garments, more layers are applied in the areas of shading. Various tones are used for this, enriching the texture of the illustration. After this step, the illustration is left to dry completely before continuing.

In this step, the shading on the clothes is added. To do this, first the areas that receive less light in the composition need to be identified. These are painted with a thick brush in darker tones than the garment, in order to create depth.

Once it has dried, the last details are drawn with a fairly fine brush, which is used like a pencil. To represent the highlights on the bag, a white gouache can be used instead of the watercolor. The details on the face are also drawn in.

Last, details like the shading on the boots, the texture of the leggins, the zipper chain, and last shadows of the bag are done; the pattern on the shirt is finished; and the eyes and mouth of the figure are painted to give the face an expression.

Pastels

Pastels are composed of chalk mixed with pigment and a binding agent, whose level of hardness depends on the proportions of these elements. Being an opaque material, it can be applied over the top of all types of surfaces painted with watercolors, gouache, acrylic, or India ink. It is a technique that can accurately represent the creases in fabric, volumes, and changes in depth. The most common formats are crayons (bars of brightly colored pastels that are easy to manipulate) and pencils (harder than crayons and ideal for detailed work). The main support for pastels is thick, textured paper, and its accessories are the stump—a tool made from paper closely rolled up, which has the thickness of a pencil, and is used for smudging—and a knife—used to sharpen the pastels to draw details. Erasers are also used. Not just to erase but also to create highlights and lights—and fixative in aerosol form or hair spray is used to protect and set the work once finished.

Aleksandra Budnik

The childhood of this Belarusian was surrounded by batiks, sculptures and embroidery, so it was natural that her higher education lead her to art school and subsequently a post-grad degree at the prestigious National University of Art of Belarus. After an intense preparation, she attained a place there to study fashion design. During the five years of the course she developed women's collections, one of which was shown in the Lafayette Galleries in Berlin, participated in several competitions, and during the last two years designed and created wedding dresses. In 2006, she graduated as one of the top students, which earned her a grant to study for a year at the Istituto Europeo di Design (IED) in Barcelona, the city where she lives today.

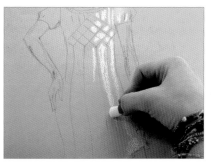

The figure is drawn on colored paper, so that the white of the dress and its lightness stand out better. The light and shade on the body are drawn with different tones, and the dress is then painted white, avoiding the fold and cut lines.

The darker shading from the ribs and the folds of the dress is done using a color that is darker than the background, such as brown, without smudging. The color of the paper, which can be seen through the dress, will be the medium tone of the shading.

A sky-blue pastel is used to accentuate the areas of shadow, which is then smudged using a finger. A fine pencil is used for the smaller details, in this case a propelling pencil. The embossed stitching around the bust, the pleats of the material, and the folds at the neck are then added.

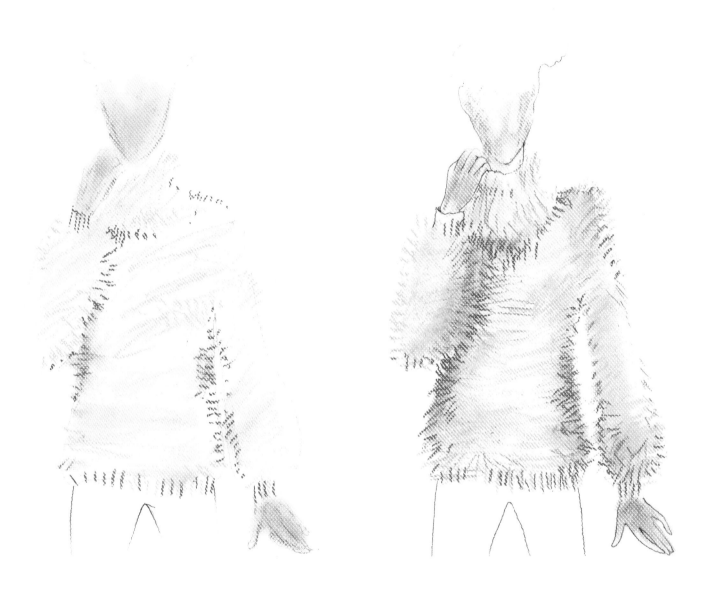

Mohair is a material with a furry texture, which is very soft and shiny. Textured paper is used to reproduce these characteristics. The figure is sketched with a pencil and then horizontal pastel lines are drawn directly onto the paper, which are smudged with a finger.

For the fur of the mohair, short strokes are used in different tones of green throughout the surface of the jersey, changing their direction for the sleeves and the neck. These lines provide greater volume and bring the garment to life.

The jersey is colored with different tones within the range of lilacs, blues, and sky-blues, to create the lights and shading and give the fabric consistency. Final details such as the ribbing on the sleeves and neck are done with fine lines in dark green.

In this case, the pastel is used in different ways. First, the skirt and its folds are drawn—and to give the base color of the skirt a dry pastel—is then grated with a craft knife onto the surface of the paper. This is then spread with a wet brush, marking out the folds in the skirt.

For the tartan pattern, the pleats of the material and how these affect the design must be taken into consideration; the lines are neither continuous nor straight between one fold and another. Then color is applied with the base color of the skirt, avoiding the lines of the tartan pattern.

Different shades of the colors from the tartan are used to create the lights and shading with pastel pencils or fine pointed pastel crayons. On the pleats of the skirt, a deep blue color is used for the shading created by these folds.

The coat is drawn, incorporating details like pockets and buttons. To achieve the effect of the frock coat material, the texture of a thick material is used, such as linen. This is placed beneath the paper to which color is applied heavily.

The outline of the coat and the sleeves is smudged with the finger to create the main volume. With a dark brown, fine-pointed pastel, details like the buttons and buttonholes, folds, creases, or stitching are drawn and then lightly smudged.

The same details are enhanced with a dark red, which creates subtler and more precise shading. The face is sketched and the silhouette is defined with brown. Any variation in the form can be easily corrected with an eraser.

The outline of the head with the neckerchief is drawn. Details are not drawn, only the folds that the neckerchief will have. The entire surface is covered with the base color of the neckerchief, which is then carefully smudged with fingers.

The pattern, in this case paisley, is drawn with colored pastels. It is important to bear in mind that the pattern follows the folds and volumes of the material, which must be shown when drawing.

The last step is to create the volumes. To do this, the lights are represented using a white pastel or one lighter than the base color, and with a pastel that is darker than the base color. The edges and knots of the neckerchief are drawn, and the folds that form the garment are added.

The figure with the sarong is drawn. With a pastel pencil the main folds are marked and lightly smudged, taking into account the direction of the light. In this case, it is from above and frontal, so the upper section and the parts that project outwards are the lighter areas.

To reproduce all the different shades created by the light and the transparencies, a wide range of colors is needed. First of all the creases in the material are drawn with a dark color, in this case, a dark blue. Then the different shades can be added.

For the different tones of the sarong, light colors are used within the same color range, like blue, sky-blue, and violet. To reproduce the transparency of the material, pink, yellow, and beige is used, which insinuate the body beneath the sarong.

Since most earmuffs come in light colors, dark paper is used to heighten the contrast. They are drawn with white, which is then smudged. The features of the face are drawn with strong, thick lines and the hair is given color, allowing glimpses of the background.

With short, quick strokes the volume and the texture of the earmuffs are drawn. Sky-blue is used for the shading and pink and yellow for the reflections. The color of the face is completed leaving a blue background for those areas in shadow.

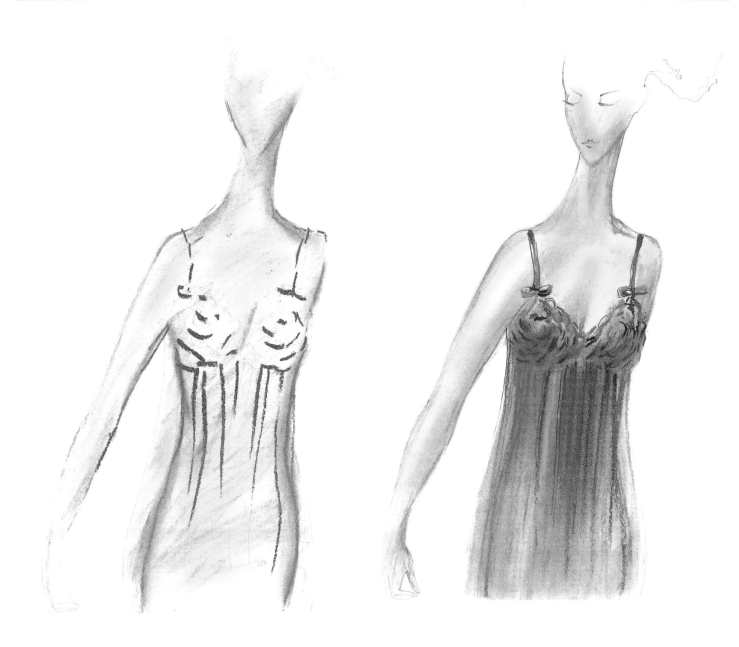

The figure is drawn and dressed in the nightdress. Because the garment is semi-transparent, first the body of the figure is colored with a skin tone. Once completed, the entire nightdress is colored pink, which will be the base color, and smudged.

To create the volume, a darker color than the base is used, in this case beige. The areas of shading are marked, like the folds, ruffles, straps, and edges of the nightdress, and then smudged. This helps to differentiate the nightdress from the color of the body.

White is used to highlight the ruffles on the upper section of the bust and some of the fold, and a magenta pencil is used to define details like the straps or the bows. A stump is used to smudge the shading beneath the chest on the lateral outline of the nightdress.

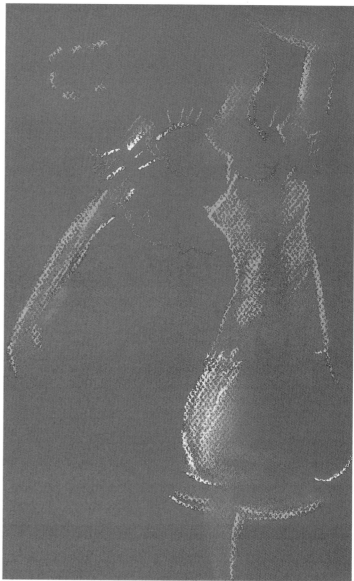

First of all, the silhouette and the elements it is composed of are drawn subtly in pencil, but without detail. The lines that mark and separate the outlines are drawn with the color that corresponds to each garment or part of the body.

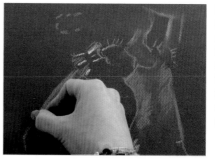

For the arms, orange and pink are used, thereby offering two tones with which to create the highlights and shading. The lines that define them are well marked, and then lightly smudged with a finger, to start to create some volume.

The waistcoat will be blue. Different tones within the range are used for this to create the highlights and shading, such as light green and black. The lines that mark the outline and the first creases are drawn and then lightly smudged.

The skirt is colored light green. Since it is a Boulloné skirt, it forms a lot of creases, which are marked in dark green. The colors of the pattern are used on the shirt, still without details, with thick, defined strokes, which are not smudged.

A little color is added to the bag (orange and red) and its texture is created. The figure will have black hair, and to create volume and a luminous effect, violet is used. Strokes are applied that follow the movement of the hair.

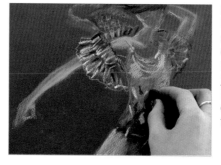

In this step, certain details like the knot on the shirt strap are defined, the line of the neck is added, the face is sketched, the folds of the jersey are gone over, the belt is drawn, and certain details of the pattern are added to make it more consistent.

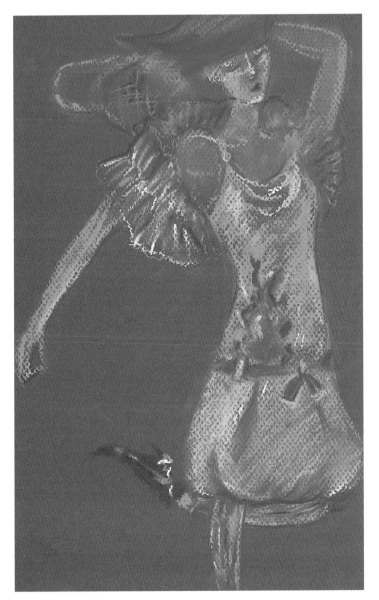

The boots and leggings are colored in detail. On the boot, white and sky-blue are applied to produce the highlight, and red is used for the stitching. To properly define the heel, its silhouette is outlined in gray. The part of the leg that is not covered by the leggings is given color.

The last details are completed, like giving the bag texture, incorporating the lights of the hair, and coloring the face to give the figure expression. For the finer details, it is recommended one to use a pencil, which allows for more thorough work.

Marker

A marker is is a writing instrument that is composed of two parts: a deposit for the ink and a tip made from a porous material, normally in felt or nylon. The tip can be different sizes and shapes. These in turn create different lines, so that each thickness has different specific use. Fine-tip markers (up to 0.157 in) are used to illustrate with great detail; medium tips (0.047 in) are ideal for illustrations made from loose and very free lines; the macro pen (0.276 in) can be used to color large surfaces quickly and evenly; and the brush pen is often used to represent both simple and highly synthesized figures and transparencies and volatile fabrics. The combination of several sizes notably enriches illustrations. It is possible to find a wide variety of colors on the market and it is a technique that can be used not just on paper but also on various surfaces such as slate, wood, plastic, etc.

Rosa Bocharán

Rosa Bocharán was born in Ciudad Real, Spain in 1968. From an early age she has been interested in drawing, painting, and fashion, which is what lead her to study artistic drawing, design and later fashion coordination, art and technique Dress. Throughout her many years of experience she has simultaneously developed her three interests. She has created fashion collections, is part of the Associació Professional d'Il·lustradors de Catalunya (APIC), and her illustrations have been published in magazines like *Cornabou*. She has developed a very personal style in her paintings, combining different techniques such as oil paints, pencils, markers, pastels, and watercolors.

With a pencil the silhouette of the figure is drawn in the desired position, in such a way as to synthesize the volume of the top. This is done with a light pencil (HB or less) to be able to then easily erase the construction lines that will not be used.

The figure to be illustrated is drawn in detail. Each feather is drawn separately, which will later make them easier to color. It is important to note the difference in the direction of the feathers on the body to those on the neck.

A medium-tip marker is used to give the skin color, applying a base layer. Various layers are applied of the same color to give volume, until the desired tone is achieved. With a brush pen the feathers are filled in, leaving small spaces in white that illuminate the top.

More layers are applied over the feathers to create different tones of black and give texture to the top, respecting the spaces in white. The rings are colored with a gold marker and to finish the entire figure is gone over with a fine black marker (02, for instance).

The jersey on the figure is drawn with a pencil. The most pronounced creases are drawn, and the texture of the fabric is sketched with lines. Because it has thick stitching, the ribbing is drawn wide, giving the material the appearance of being heavy.

Two tones from the same range are used to color the jersey. A first layer is applied with each color to give a base tone, leaving small spaces of white, which illuminate the composition. Over this layer the outline of the belt is drawn.

Several layers of each color are applied to create volumes. For the more intense shading, a darker violet is used. The furry effect is achieved by stippling with a marker, and the lines of the ribbing are marked with a black fine-tip marker.

The entire figure is outlined with a black fine-tip marker (02). The jersey outline is marked with a wobbly line to simulate the furry texture of the jersey. The buckle and the button holes of the belt are drawn and the creases are added.

The silhouette of the body is drawn, standing up and leaning over one of the hips. The basic forms and volumes of the skirt are drawn over the figure in pencil. No detail is drawn, just the different layers and cuts of the material.

The skirt is drawn over the basic figure, marking the movements and undulations of the fabric. The pleats in this fine material produce many folds and creases, which should be marked in detail. The lines previously drawn are erased.

With a medium-tip marker, a first layer of each color is applied. In this case, black and crimson have been chosen. Color is applied evenly but while spaces are left to mark the lights and divisions.

Several layers of the same color are applied with the marker to achieve darker tones and thus create the corresponding shading. Finally the edges and folds are outlined with a black fine-tip marker (02).

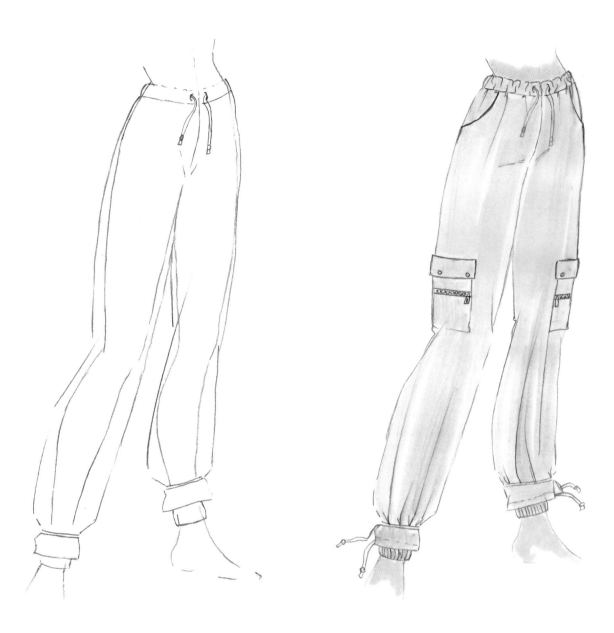

The silhouette of the figure is drawn with a light pencil (HB or less) and the shape of the trousers is drawn on top of this. Certain constructive details are drawn, like the cut of the fabric and the waistband of the belt and the feet, as well as the cord for adjusting the trousers.

Still with the pencil, the figure is better defined. The pockets and their zips are drawn, the creases are marked, and detail is drawn on the lower part of the trousers. Next, a first layer is applied with a marker, leaving spaces of white for the light.

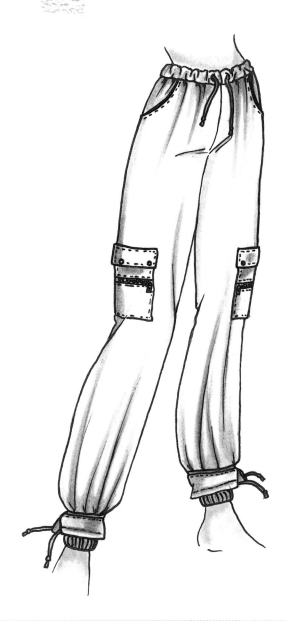

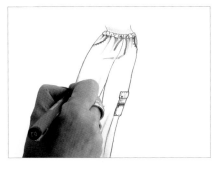

To create the shading of the creases, several layers of color are applied to the base color of the trousers. The upper and lower section is given more color, which is where the creases are most concentrated, leaving the central area clearer. The details are marked with a fine-tip marker.

The coat is drawn with a soft pencil. To create the guides for applying color, the buttons, the details of the belt, the shoulders, and the sleeve and the marks of the creases formed by the position of the material, are all drawn in detail.

A wide-tip marker is used to apply an even layer of red, to provide the base color. Some areas are left white to give light to the garment. With a black fine-tip marker the lines of the tartan are drawn, following the form and movement of the fabric.

Several layers are applied to achieve the areas of shading, which give the garment volume. A darker tone can also be used for this. The black lines of the pattern are completed and given detail, and then the backstitches are marked with a white marker.

The figure is drawn in pencil in the desired posture. Because the leggings are going to be illustrated, the most recommended posture is one with one leg in front of the other to be able to clearly see the design. The silhouette of the leggings is marked, which being lycra has no creases or folds.

The geometric pattern is drawn, taking into account that the form of the body and its movements must be followed, hence straight lines are avoided. An initial base layer is applied with each color, leaving white spaces for the light and divisions.

To achieve darker tones, several layers of each color are applied until the desired tones are obtained. Being lycra, the color is quite even, so only volume on the legs is marked. For better definition, the drawing is outlined with a fine-tip marker.

A flat drawing of the sneaker is done without details, only marking the main lines that separate one color from another. A soft pencil is used in case anything needs to be erased, and so that there are no marks and the result is clean.

Three colors are used for the sneaker: red, dark gray, and a very light gray to then make the shading from the white. With a wide-tip marker a layer of each color is applied, and, being an opaque material, white spaces are not left for the highlights.

More layers of color are applied until the desired tones are achieved. For the white areas, few layers are applied, thus avoiding overly intense shading and generating little volume. The trainer and the details are outlined with a fine-tip marker (02).

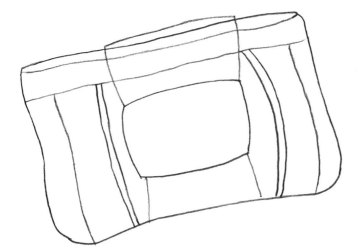

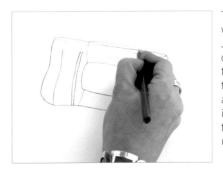

The bag is drawn in pencil without too much detail. Just the volume it will occupy, the cuts between the different materials, and the position of the clasp are drawn. A soft pencil is used so that afterward the lines that will not be used are not shown.

Color is applied using the base colors of the bag, leaving spaces of white, which give light to the drawing. Various layers are applied to create the initial volumes. The clasp is painted with a gold fine-tip marker and the folds and shading are marked with a brush pen.

With a black fine-tip marker (02), the details of the bag are marked: the lines of the creases and the stitching are drawn, and the edges are outlined. With a white fine-tip marker small lines are made on the clasp to give it light.

With a soft pencil the figure is drawn in the desired pose. Then, with a darker pencil, the main garments are drawn—ribbed woolen waistcoat, shirt, Boulloné skirt, and boots—simply, and only marking the volumes.

The final details are drawn, which will serve as a guide when coloring with the marker: the pattern on the shirt; the frames of the glasses; the zipper, the chain and the clips of the bag; the leggings; the zipper on the boots; and the folds of the skirt and the waistcoat.

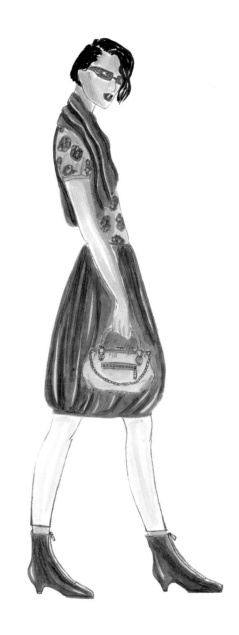

A layer is applied with the base colors of each garment, leaving small spaces of white for the lighter areas. A brush pen is used for the hair, which achieves a better texture. The leggings are given a skin color since they will be semi-transparent.

Various layers of the base color are applied to each garment to achieve darker shades. The shading is created and lighter areas are left, which in turn form the volumes of the garments. It is important not to color over the spaces left white.

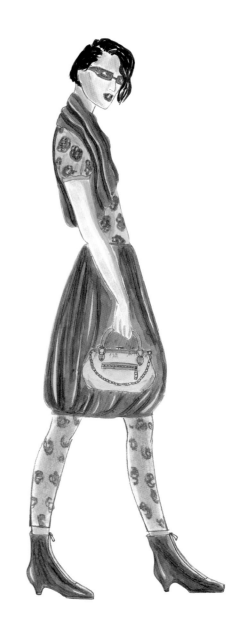

To achieve the transparency of the leggings, the marker is used in combination with a pastel, a technique that allows this effect to be better illustrated. A black pastel is used to draw a light layer. This should then be smudged with a cotton swab.

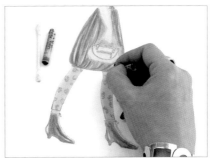

The pastel is used again for the details of the pattern on the leggings. A slightly darker tone is used than that obtained for the base, in this case violet. The movement of the legs should be taken into account when drawing the motifs.

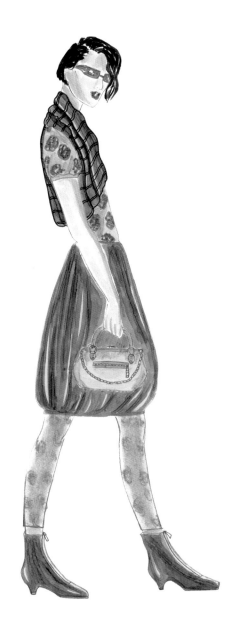

The details of each garment are marked. To create the texture of the waistcoat a fine marker is used (02). The lines that represent the ribbing are drawn, taking into account that these are not straight or even, but follow the movement of the garment.

With the black marker, the main creases formed in the skirt are marked, the padded texture of the bag is created (and its details are drawn in) the zip on the boots is drawn, the facial features are added, and lastly the entire figure is outlined.

Gouache

Gouache or tempera has been used since medieval times, at which time it was known as temple paint. It is often confused with watercolors, since both techniques are applied in a similar manner. The difference, however, is that gouache is heavier and more opaque. It is applied using layers and veils (diluted). And, in contrast with watercolors, the darker tones can be applied first or over these the lighter ones or even white. This means that despite its matte finish, it is the perfect technique for illustrating reflections and intense highlights for elements like glasses, jewelry, gems, or metals. It dries quite quickly and, once dried, errors can be corrected by superimposing layers, bearing in mind that if the layer is too thick it may crack. The materials used for this technique are: a heavy paper, recipients with water, a palette for mixing the colors, and brushes of different thickness, depending on the level of detail that needs to be achieved.

Loreto Binvignat

Originally from La Serena, Chile, she lived in several cities during her childhood—both inside and outside of the country—giving her a more open vision of the world. On returning to Chile, she finished high school and studied art at the Pontificia Universidad Católica, which marked the beginning of her artistic career, and hopes of continuing her training in New York or Europe. After two years, she moved to the Dominican Republic to study fashion design in the Altos de Chavón School, affiliated to the Parsons School of Design in New York. After the first term, she decided to continue her studies in Barcelona, graduating at the Istituto Europeo di Design (IED). Today she works as a fashion designer for an international company and as a freelance illustrator.

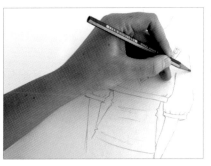

A light pencil (HB or less) is used to draw the top, so that this does not dominate the drawing. All the details are drawn, and for the gems it is recommended one draw the faces of each stone, in order to follow the forms and highlights when coloring.

The blue base color of the top is painted with a thick brush. The advantage of the gouache is that if the result is not even, it can be corrected by adding one or more layers afterward. The base color of the skin is also applied in this step, which will be finished off later.

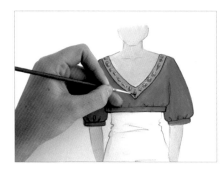

Color is applied to the base where the strip of gems will be, which are then evenly painted. With a very fine brush, the highlights are added to different parts of each stone, depending on the direction of the light. Last, the main folds and shading are marked with gray.

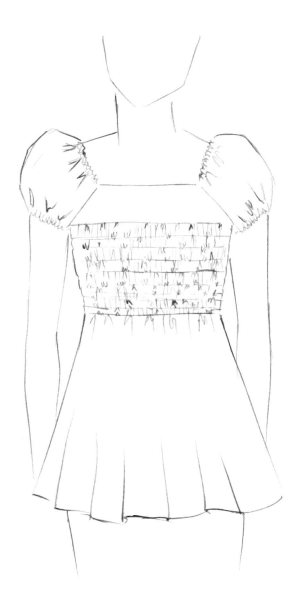

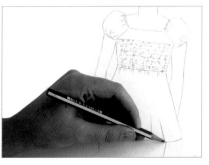

The shirt is drawn in pencil. In the ribbed area it is not necessary to draw all the creases but rather to synthesize and mark only some of them. It is recommended that one make some blacker than others to create depth. This will serve as a guide when it comes to applying color.

With a reasonably thick brush, the first layers of each color are applied, with the gouache very diluted in water, thus obtaining a lighter tone for each color. This is done flatly and evenly without consideration for the light or shading.

With a less dilute gouache the stitching and creases formed by the ribs and the sleeves are marked. Because the material is cotton and does not create reflections, it will not be necessary to add white for the points of light. For a better finish, the edge is outlined with a pencil or marker.

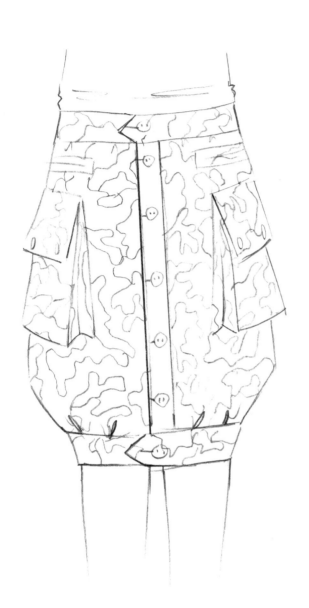

With a light marker the skirt is drawn with all its constructive details. Then the organic forms of the military pattern are drawn, taking into account that the part where the buttons are will not be patterned and that the material changes direction at the pockets.

The lighter of the three colors in the pattern is used as the base color for the skirt. It is applied with a thick brush in large strokes, keeping it even so that the tone is the same for the entire surface.

Based on the original army colors, the other two shades of green are chosen for the pattern. The application of these colors follows the pattern that has been drawn. To be able to follow it exactly, a brush of medium thickness is used.

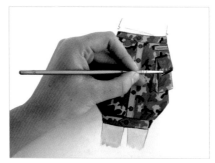

To finish, black is applied, the tone that is darkest and has least presence. The black areas of the pattern are colored and a marker is used for the details like the edges of the buttons and pockets or the creases in the skirt.

The skirt is drawn with a light pencil (HB or less). The main creases and the stripes from the pattern are added. When drawing these it is important to remember that where there are folds the stripes become curved and do not follow the exterior line.

A medium brush, between 6 and 10, is used to apply the base color of the skin and the red from the stripes. A good way to obtain a more detailed result for the stripes is to position the paper diagonally, so that the wrist can follow its natural movement.

The stripes that may not have been correctly painted can be defined with a thick layer. To create depth in the interior of the folds, the red stripes are painted in a less diluted color, and a grayish veil is applied to the white stripes.

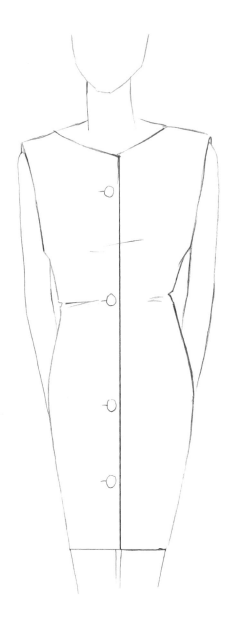

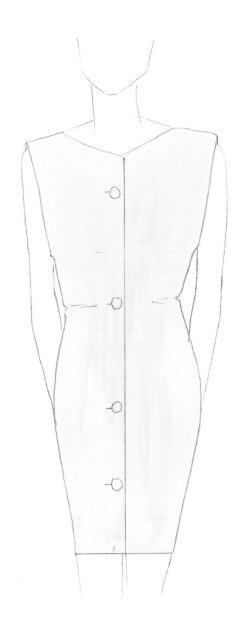

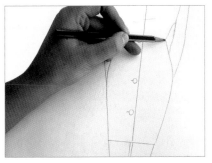

The dress is drawn simply, only marking the buttons, the cut, and the main creases. It is not necessary to draw the pattern or the patches, as they will be done in a more random way, which will also allow the colors and the forms to stand out more.

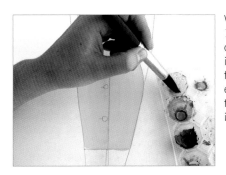

With a thick brush, between 16 and 20, the first layer of yellow is applied, which is the dominant color of the fabric. It must be applied as evenly as possible to be able to create the pattern cleanly in the next steps.

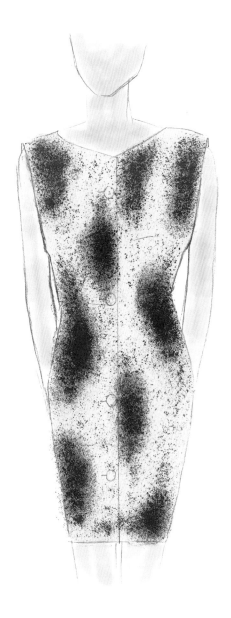
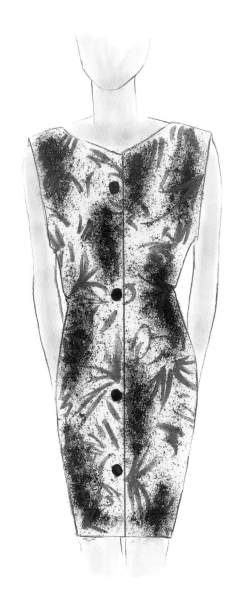

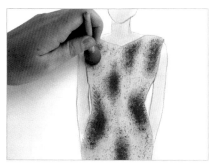

To create the smudged effect, a small sponge dipped in a thick layer of red is used. It is then stamped onto the dress, first heavily and then more gently to create the smudged effect between the patches.

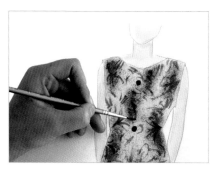

To finish, the organic motifs are painted randomly on the previously colored surface. Then the final details are added, like painting the buttons and going over the outline of the figure with a pencil to improve the definition.

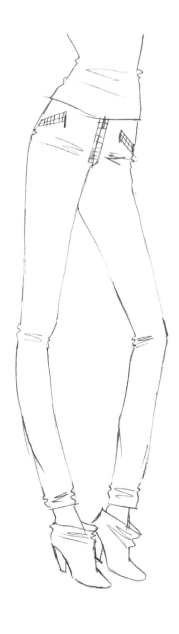

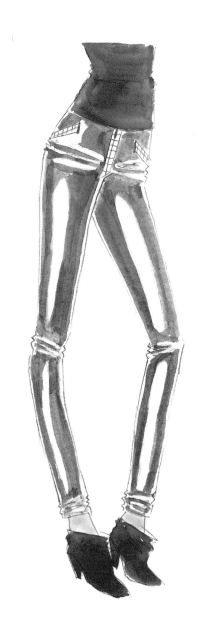

The trousers are drawn with a soft pencil, so that the work is left clean in case anything needs to be erased. The creases in the trousers are drawn formed by the inclined posture of the figure. The creases in the shoes, the zipper, and the pockets are also added.

The medium tones are applied and the shading and highlights are outlined. For the trousers, first a thin, grayish layer is applied, which will be the middle tone of the gradation from the white to the black. The area with highlights is left completely white.

Layers of dark colors are added, leaving areas of gradation so that the shine seems more real. If some of the color passes onto the areas where there are total highlights, where the paper is meant to be left white, these can be easily corrected with a thick white gouache.

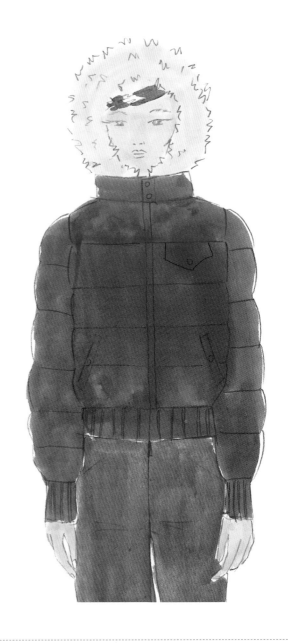

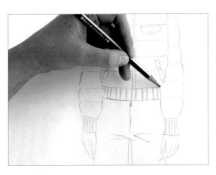

The figure is drawn with a light pencil. To represent the volume of the fur from the hood, small lines are drawn around this section. It is important when drawing the silhouette of the parka to reflect its volume, which can be achieved with curved lines.

To achieve the lightest tones of each color, a fairly diluted gouache is used to apply an initial layer in orange for the body of the parka and beige for the furry hood. On this base, darker tones can be applied to create the shading.

A second layer is applied with the less diluted gouache, and therefore this darker layer begins to give volume to the fur on the hood and to the body. To add volume and depth in the fur, small lines are applied in different sizes and tones.

The last step is to add the shading. To obtain darker tones, orange is mixed with red and beige with brown. These colors are used for the respective darker areas of the parka, such as the stitching and the details of the fur.

With a light pencil (HB or less) the face and glasses are drawn. Details like the cheekbones, the lips, and the motif on the glasses are drawn. The areas with highlights can be marked with a very light 3H pencil to provide a guide when it comes to applying color.

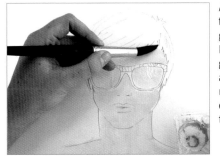

An initial skin tone is applied throughout the face with the gouache fairly watered down. Because the lenses of the glasses are transparent, the area they occupy should also receive the same skin color, except for the areas where there are highlights.

With a very diluted black gouache, which will actually be seen as gray, an initial layer is painted to define the shading and highlights. The black part of the frames is painted with a thicker, and therefore darker, gouache to differentiate them from the lenses, and the fuchsia and blue are both applied.

Definition is given to the drawing by applying more layers of each color and perfecting the details. The highlights and reflections in the lenses are outlined with white, and small white lines are drawn on the frames. For a better finish, the face is outlined in pencil.

With the base of all the colors done, the details of the garments are started. A layer of shading is applied to the outline of the waistcoat and with a very fine brush and in a darker tone the lines of the ribbing are drawn along with small spikes to simulate the fabric.

A very fine brush—number 0 to 1—is used to give color to the glasses, which will make it easier to paint them accurately. First, a gray veil is applied to the lenses, leaving the highlights white. Then the black frames are painted very carefully.

The other elements are painted black. The hair is done with small brush strokes, following its natural direction. With a 0 pencil the stitching on the bag is outlined and each cheek is given color. The highlight is left white, as in the case with the boots.

Now, definition is given to all the elements—details on the pattern, the volume of the waistcoat and skirt, and the facial expression—and darker tones and the brightest highlights are applied. Finally, the figure is outlined with a pencil or marker.

Mixed Techniques and Digital Illustration

Mixed techniques refer to both illustrations that combine techniques already seen and collages. The advantage of these is that by using pieces of material, paper, thread, sequins, etc. the combination of textures and materials found in an outfit can be better presented and the final result more closely represents the garments themselves. All the mixed technique illustrations have been done by hand, making each result unique. Digital illustration is illustration work that uses a computer in part or all of the process. Drawings can be scanned and colored afterward using a computer, different images can be scanned and then mixed, or one can draw directly onto the computer with a "digital pencil" on a monitor. The main programs that are used are Photoshop and Illustrator. The advantage that this technique offers is that tests of color and form can be carried out on a single illustration, until reaching a satisfactory result.

Daria Jabenko | www.illustrationweb.com   // *Mixed Techniques*

Unified by a romantic touch, each illustration presents its own personality. They combine gouache, watercolors, and ink to achieve high levels of detail. The harmonious color palette is dominated by different shades of red.

Zulema Galeano | www.zulema.org   // *Digital*

The base for these illustrations is old paper, which is drawn on and colored with pencils, markers, ballpoints, or watercolors. Then color is applied using Photoshop, or a filter is used (such as the mosaic in the case of the skirt) which helps to create unique pieces.

Olivia Rubin | www.oliviarubinlondon.com

// Digital

To achieve a representation that is as close as possible to the garments of this designer, the figures—drawn in pencil and colored with watercolors—are scanned and, in Photoshop, the patterns and textures are applied.

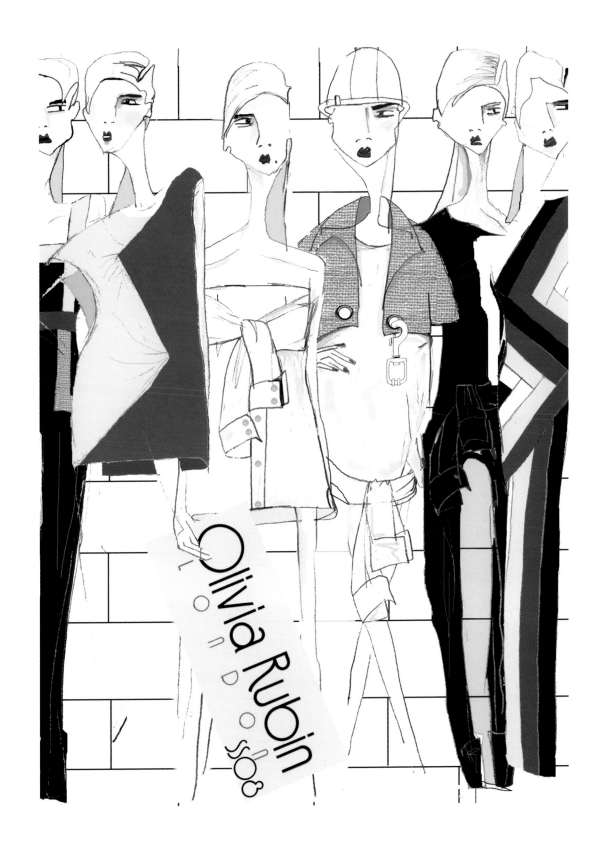

Carolina Alonso Lavalle | caroalonva@yahoo.com   // Collage

To enliven these compositions, done entirely by hand, different elements have been combined such as cuttings from magazines, cloth, and dressmaking materials like wool or sequins. The designs play with color contrasts, textures, and patterns.

Marisa Fjärem | www.fjarem.com/marisa   *// Collage*

The aim of these illustrations is to show the clothes without using the idealized figure of a model. They have been created using paper cuttings—similar to the cloth from the garments both in structure and in color—combined with drawings and photos.

Paula Sanz Caballero | www.paulasanzcaballero.com — // Collage

Each piece is sewn entirely by hand, which is a slow and meticulous task. When doing this, the intrinsic qualities of the materials are not taken into account but are taken to their limits to achieve the creative aims.

Maria Cardelli | www.mariacardelli.com   *// Digital*

These digitally created collages are given life through the variety of materials, such as enamel paints, oils, papers, or anything that could afford an interesting texture. They are then combined on the computer to create visually striking compositions.

ΜΑΡΤΙΟΣ 2007 / FASHION & THE CITY LOOK MAGAZINE ΤΕΥΧΟΣ 13 / FREE PRESS

LO**mag**

DÉFILES

SS'07

H MARIA CARDELLI
σχεδιάζει το εξώφυλλο
του LOOKmag

Sarah Beetson/Illustration Ltd | www.illustrationweb.com/SarahBeetson   *// Collage*

Diverse materials, such as spray paint, tissue paper, and circular stickers, have been combined to create these colorful illustrations, which have been applied over drawings made with pens, wax pencils, and markers.

Chris Ede/Illustration Ltd | www.illustrationweb.com   // *Digital*

First a sketch of the composition is done and then the elements are drawn separately with ink, acrylics, and watercolors. These are scanned and, in Photoshop, color, texture and perhaps the odd effect are applied to create the final illustration.

LAU* | www.laura-mc.com

// Digital

The technique used in these illustrations combines black ink, markers, and Photoshop. Flat colors were chosen along with geometric motifs to achieve quick results, where the line of the figures and objects is accentuated.

PPaint | www.ppaint.net

// Digital

The figure is drawn with a brush, pencil, or pen, and the other elements are painted and treated to create textures. This is all scanned, mounted, and colored, using few effects so that the final illustration, although digital, does not appear artificial.

1

Sophie Leblanc | sofk.free.fr   // *Digital*

The initial drawing is done by hand and afterward a computer is used to apply colors, graphic streams, and textures. These come from magazine cuttings and snippets of cloth, which are scanned, thus bringing a high level of realism to the illustrations.

4

1
2
3
4 ✗
5

6

5

4, 5 and 6: Illustrations extracted from *La Mode* by Gentiane Lenhard, illustrated by Nikita, Sophie Leblanc © 2007 Éditions Milan

Oscar Giménez | www.oscargimenez.com

// Digital

The initial line is always drawn in pencil, then on the computer the line is polished and the rest of the illustration is done on Photoshop. Color ranges that do not form excessive contrasts are often used and it is common to integrate real textures with photographic elements.

Bjørn Brochmann/Commando Group | www.commandogroup.com

// Digital

Photoshop is the main tool here. Flatter illustrations can be achieved, such as those that combine drawings done with ink and hand-written letters, or more realist compositions, such as those that mix parts of photos with lines from the same photos.

Carole Agaësse | www.caroleagaesse.com

// Digital

The Bézier curve is a digitally drawn shape based on the insertion of control points that allow the curvature of the line to be adjusted. These illustrations use them to obtain perfect outlines around the figures and the patterns.

Mariya Paskovsky | www.mpaskovsky.com

// Digital

The pictures are hand drawn and then given color using Photoshop, which can combine gradients, flat inks, and real textures in the compositions. They are modern illustrations but have decorative elements that are reminiscent of art nouveau and popular art.

1

Kun-Sung Chung | www.kschung.com

// Digital

Illustrator CS2 has been used from start to finish to create these illustrations. Most of them use just three tools: pen, gradient, and transparencies. Inspired by the concept "less is more," filters and effects have been avoided where possible.

2

1 and 2: Illustrations © Kun-Sung Chung / www.kschung.com

3

G.G. Book by Wendy Roy

4

Inoue Taiji | mooz.com.br/rti9

// Digital

To create these illustrations, first the figures are drawn in pencil and then scanned. Once digitalized, the color is applied. Flat inks are used for this and different shades are combined in a single garment to create volume.

nando&silvia/potipoti Graphic Division | www.potipoti.com   // Digital

This is an unconventional and fun way of illustrating fashion, where the classic figure is not used. Drawings done using markers are combined with pieces created in Freehand, which allows for the creation of different motifs on the garments.

Avsh Alom Gur | www.avshalomgur.com   *// Collage*

This is a particular style that salvages a classical, low-tech piece of equipment: the photocopier. A photograph is introduced, which is copied as a negative, and during the process the tray is drawn on to create movement. The finishing touches are done with markers.

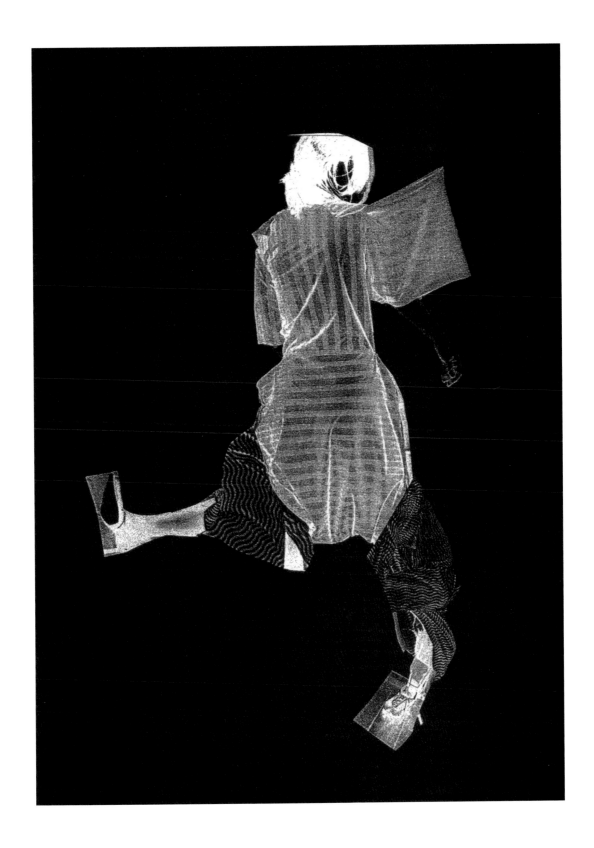